ALL IS WELL

FRANK E. PERETTI

WORD PUBLISHING

Dallas·London·Vancouver·Melbourne

All Is Well

Library of Congress-in-Publication Data

Peretti, Frank E.
    All Is Well : A Christmas Story / by Frank E. Peretti :
       illustrated by Robert Sauber.
         p.   cm.
     "Word kids!"
        Summary: Poverty stricken and low on hope. A
divorced mother and her daughter prop up their sagging
spirits and keep the flames of faith alive by clinging to a phrase
first heard on a previous Christmas, "All is well."

  ISBN 0-8499-0918-X
     [1. Christian life--Fiction. 2. Christmas--Fiction.]
    I. Sauber, Rob, ill. II. Title.
    PZ7.p4254A1   1991
    [Fic]--dc20   91 - 29625
                                      CIP
                                         AC

Managing editor: Laura Minchew. Project editor: Brenda Ward

Printed in the United States of America
1239LB987654321
Printed by Lake Book Manufacturing, Inc.

ALL IS WELL

To all the single moms:
> *You've got your work cut out for you.*
> *Here's some hope to take along.*

Frank E. Peretti

All is well. Because God entered our world as a child born in a manger, all is well.

We all know that . . . well, sort of. I mean, "All Is Well" would make a nice plaque on the wall or a nice greeting. It's kind of like: "God Is Good" or "In All Things Give Thanks."

But . . . "All Is Well?" Do we always see it that way? At Christmastime we act like we believe it, but all too often as far as we can see, nothing is well.

I guess it depends on where you're standing and how good the view is from there.

That's how it was for Ruth Preston and her little daughter, Jenny.

It was July — no snow, no tinsel, nothing but the real world no matter where you looked. It had been almost two years since the divorce, and Ruth and Jenny's last Christmas had been a flop. Ruth still didn't want to think about Christmas or anything connected with it — nothing, that is, except that little phrase, "All is well." She had first heard the phrase at Christmastime many years ago, and for some reason it had stuck in her memory. Now she held onto that phrase. She needed something to keep their spirits up, to keep their hopes alive.

"Mom, didn't you buy any Cheerios®?" asked Jenny, as her mother returned from the grocery store. "No," said Ruth, "but look at it this way: We saved money, and I didn't have to carry as much stuff home. I didn't have to carry Cheerios or ice cream or popcorn or cocoa or dish soap either. Just feel how light this grocery bag is!"

"Yeah, nice and light and easy to carry!" said Jenny, trying to go along with her mom.

"So all is well, right?" Ruth asked her daughter.

"All is well," Jenny answered, barely above a whisper.

"I think I heard an answer . . ." Ruth said, holding her hand to her ear.

"All is well!" Jenny responded with lively determination.

"That's the stuff! It won't be long now before I'll be getting a raise at work."

"What does that mean?"

"It means things are gonna be better." Ruth tried to sound hopeful.

"Then can you go back to nursing school?" asked Jenny.

"Well . . . no. I'll still have to work to pay the bills. Besides, I don't need that old nursing school anyway."

"I could work," Jenny offered, eager to help out.

"Thanks. But you're too little."

"I could sell stuff."

"Honey, we've already sold everything that isn't nailed down."

"But Mom . . . we gotta have faith, remember?"

"That's what I've always said," Ruth agreed.

"So, can I?" Jenny asked, but her mother was thinking about other things.

"Did we get any mail?" Ruth wanted to know.

"I put it on your dresser," said Jenny.

Ruth hoped that perhaps there would be a child-support check today from Jenny's Dad.

No, not today. Ruth opened the envelope and frowned.

"What is it, Mom?"

"It's . . . well, it's a letter from our landlord."

"Is he mad?"

"Oh, he's . . . well, we'll make it." Ruth's words were as much to convince herself as they were to encourage Jenny.

"All is well," said Jenny.

"All . . . is well!" Ruth repeated with more hope than she felt.

"So, can I?" Jenny pleaded.

"Can you what?" asked her mother.

"Sell stuff."

Ruth said yes.

Early on Saturday the neighbors could hear the rumble and squeak of Jenny's wagon as she went from house to house. Timidly she knocked at every door.

"Hi. I'm Jenny Preston. I'm buying and selling stuff."

Abby Duvall, the plumber's wife, was still in her bathrobe. She hadn't had her coffee, and now the light of day was making her squint.

"What are you selling? Looks like junk!"

"It's good junk. Look at this."

"A coffee can?"

"You can keep things in it. Look, it's so shiny on the bottom you can see yourself in it."

Mrs. Duvall laughed. "I don't need any more empty cans around here!"

"I've got an egg carton for keeping jewelry or buttons
or small things," said Jenny.
"No, said Mrs. Duvall."
Jenny opened a small box full of mismatched, tangled,
old and new, from-here-and-there, sparkly surprises.
"How about some Christmas ornaments?"
"In July?"
"Buy 'em now, use 'em later."

Mrs. Duvall did take a moment to paw through the box, but she finally shook her curlered head. "Naw, I don't need to be thinking about Christmas. I've got enough problems."

"Don't you like Christmas?"

"Some need it, some don't. Hey, did you say you're buying stuff too?"

"Yes, ma'am."

"Well, hang on."

Mrs. Duval left Jenny standing at the door. When she came back, she had what looked like a wooden candlestick . . . or maybe it was a spindle or table leg, or . . .

"I got this at a white-elephant party. I'll take a dollar for it."

Jenny bit her lip. "Well . . . I haven't sold anything yet. Maybe after I sell something I can come back . . . "

Mrs. Duvall laughed. "Here. Maybe you can get a dollar for it."

"Wow! Thanks!"

"Good luck."

The rest of the morning didn't go much better. Junk seemed to be something everybody had plenty of and no one needed to buy.

"God, you just gotta help me sell something. I don't want Mom to be sad," Jenny prayed.

Honk honk!

It was Mr. Patrick in his old red truck. Jenny waved

hello because Mr. Patrick always waved back.

     This time he pulled to a stop and rolled down his window.

     "Hi there, Jenny!"

     "Hi, Mr. Patrick!"

     Mr. Patrick had white frizzy hair and a round, red nose. He would have made a good Santa Claus. He liked kids, too; he'd always let Jenny and her friends cross his yard to get to the woods.

"What do you have there in the wagon?"

"I'm buying and selling special things today. Wanna take a look?"

Mr. Patrick parked his truck and got out. He was dirty; he'd been digging ditches for the county again.

"I've got a shiny coffee can and a nice egg carton."

"What's this thing here?"

"Mom used to open jars with it."

"But it's broken . . . "

"Yes, sir, I know. But you can scratch your back with it—like this. See?" Jenny showed Mr. Patrick just how it would work.

"Very clever. What's in the box?"

"Oh . . . that's Christmas stuff. I guess it's the wrong time of the year. Nobody wants to buy it."

"Eh, let me see it."

Jenny opened the box, and the sunlight danced across the silver and gold sparkles. Mr. Patrick carefully picked up each piece: a toy soldier, a teddy bear, a silver star.

He must have seen something that touched his heart. Jenny could see it in his face.

"I'll give you ten dollars for the whole box," said Mr. Patrick.

Jenny couldn't even talk—her eyes and mouth were wide open. Mr. Patrick pulled out a crinkled bill and put it in Jenny's hand. "Merry Christmas."

"Ten dollars! Wait till I show Mom!"

To Jenny ten dollars seemed like a fortune, but her mom knew it wouldn't go very far toward paying the overdue bills. It wouldn't fill the empty cupboards or pay the rent either.

"Oh, Jenny! That's just wonderful!" Ruth tried to sound cheerful. But her eyes were red and Jenny knew she'd been crying.

"What's the matter, Mom?"

"Oh, nothing! Nothing! We're doing great, and you're really being helpful! Ten dollars! Wow!"

"So . . . all is well?"

"You bet, Jenny, all is well!"

But Jenny couldn't feel good. She could only stare at her mother's sad face.

"Mom, tell me how come."

"How come what?"

"How come all is well?"

Ruth sighed and rested her elbows on the desk.

"Jenny, it just is. We just believe that. We have to believe that."

"But you always used to tell me how come, every

Christmas. Remember?"

     "Well, of course, I remember," Ruth told herself. "It was because . . . it was just that . . ." Well, she'd had so much on her mind lately. And it was a long time ago.

     Truthfully, Ruth didn't remember. She just sat there and couldn't say a word. She could feel the blood drain from her face.

     Jenny must have seen it because she reached and touched her mother's hand.

"Mom—" she said, then stopped suddenly. Jenny had remembered something. "Oh no . . ." she gasped. Quickly Jenny turned and ran out the door.

"Jenny, where— Don't— Jenny!"

Too late. Jenny was gone, not looking back. Ruth felt terrible.

There was something Jenny had to find. First she looked in the storage shed out back. Then she went through the boxes left over from the yard sale. She even pawed through some of the trash, but she couldn't find it. It must have been in the box she sold to Mr. Patrick.

Jenny grabbed her wagon and pulled it down the street clickety clack to Mr. Patrick's house.

The pleasant old man came to the door as soon as Jenny knocked.

"Mr. Patrick, please, I need to buy back one of those Christmas things. It was . . . a little dangly thing on a string, and it had glittery letters on it . . . "

"The little clay one?"

"That's it!"

"Oh Jenny, I'm sorry, I don't have that anymore. I gave it to Mrs. Peringer. She . . . well, she's been having some rough times lately, and I thought it might encourage her a bit."

"Mrs. Peringer?"

"That green house over there with the rail fence."

Jenny ran to Mrs. Peringer's house pulling the wagon behind her.

"Mrs. Peringer, I need to buy something back. It's a little dangly thing on a string, and it's made of clay, and—"

Mrs. Peringer had the most peaceful smile on her face! "Mmm, I know the one you're talking about. Sweetheart, I

don't have it anymore. I thought it might be a blessing to the Buxtons, so I gave it to them."

Jenny ran to the Buxtons. They'd given it to the Dysowskis.

Jenny went to the Dysowskis, then the Jones, and then the Seversons. Up and down the street she went.

Finally she came to John Ketcham's house.

"Mr. Ketcham, I'm Jenny Preston from up the street, and I need to buy something back. I don't have any money, but here, you can have this coffee can that you can put things in. And you can have this egg carton that's good for buttons and small things, and this wooden thing that I don't know what it is, and this back scratcher . . . you can have my wagon. Just . . . please . . . I've got to have that little clay thing back!"

Jenny'd been gone for almost two hours, and Ruth wanted to go find her. But then they'd be alone, just the two of them, in their little apartment with the bare walls and peeling paint. Jenny's eyes would be asking the same question that Ruth had lost the answer for: "Mom, how come all is well?"

And what could she tell her? Just, the same old thing: All is well. Don't worry. Keep your chin up, kid. All is well—

"Oh, God! If you've given up on us, if you don't care about us anymore, then let me know right now because I can't go on acting like you do care."

Ruth didn't even hear Jenny come in.

"Mom?" Jenny's cheeks were red from running.
"Mom, I got it back."

It was a little clay Christmas ornament. Ruth took it,
turned it over a few times, and memories came flooding back.

"Jenny . . . where did you find this?"

"It was in a box with some other Christmas stuff. I accidentally sold it to Mr. Patrick, but he gave it to Mrs. Peringer. Then she gave it to the Buxtons, and . . ." Jenny had to name every stop she'd made all around the neighborhood. "And then Mr. Ketcham just gave it back to me, and he even let me keep my wagon. Now do you remember, Mom?"

Ruth remembered. Jenny made this ornament when she was five. It was misshapen, the painted colors were faded, but the message was clear.

On one side were those words: All is well.

On the other side was the reason: For unto us a child is born.

A sudden gleam of hope filled Ruth's face, and Jenny could see it. "All is well, huh, Mom?"

Ruth closed her hands around that little lump of clay and held on.

"All is well, Jenny. We just can't see it yet. But some way, somehow, all is well."

When you're the storyteller, you know things the people in your story don't know. I know why all those neighbors were passing that ornament around. They were buying it from each other to raise money for the Prestons. It was Mr. Patrick's idea, and tomorrow they'll take the money to the Prestons and holler "Merry Christmas!" — in July!

So I know Ruth and Jenny will be taken care of. And I know that eventually, Ruth will finish nursing school. And I know that things won't be easy, but they'll make it.

Ruth knows it too. No one has told her and she can't
see any of it yet. But . . . now that she remembers how come
"All is well" . . . she knows.

And she'll tell Jenny once again that God is the Grand Storyteller of our lives. She'll tell her that, in a stable in Bethlehem so long ago, God wrote Himself into history. Now He walks with us in the midst of the story, and He'll stay with us until that story is completed His way, in His time, for His glory.

And that's how come "all is well."
Remember?